CORRUPTION
IN THE NIGERIAN
PUBLIC SERVICE

NIPPING IT IN THE BUD

Emmanuel Olisa Iwobi, JP.

ISBN: Softcover   978-1-4990-8449-8
            eBook   978-1-4990-8448-1

This book was printed in the United States of America.

©Emmanuel Iwobi and Associates.
Email: odika1900@hotmail.com.
Phone: 08160380650. 07054466782.

Contemporary approach to nipping corruption in the public service, Vol. 1.

Compiled by: Emmanuel O. Iwobi.
            Ahmed Pate.
            Anjorin F. Abraham.
            Dauda Halilu.
            Daniel T. Ogunkeye.

Rev. date: 10/15/2014

To order additional copies of this book, contact:
Xlibris LLC
1-888-795-4274
www.Xlibris.com
Orders@Xlibris.com
696135

DEDICATION

*T*his handbook is dedicated to posterity to show evidence of the efforts made by this generation to break out of the web of corruption that has impoverished the majority of Nigerians, a negative legacy bequeathed to us by historical events that have made national growth and sustained development elusive. It beckons on the exertion of more efforts and determination to liberate the country from the self-imposed burden.

ACKNOWLEDGEMENT

I wish to thank God for the privilege in assigning me and my colleagues to articulate appropriate mode in disseminating relevant information on corruption in the system and effective remedies in curtailing it. It is an independent perspective drawn from long-standing experience in the system.

Commendation to my erstwhile colleagues in the Audit Unit of the Economic and Financial Crime Commission (EFCC), Mr. Ahmed Pate, Mr. Abraham Anjorin, Mr. Halilu Dauda and Mr. Daniel Ogunkeye, who contributed immensely in accomplishing this project which we all started together.

I also wish to express my gratitude to erstwhile colleague and friend in the Ministry of Foreign Affairs, Mr. Ahmed Ekpolomo for his encouragement and support which made the maiden publication possible.

Special appreciation goes to Ambassador Dr. Chijioke Wilcox Wigwe who edited the draft copy.

FOREWORD

T here is need for sensitization and awareness that will jolt every citizen to cooperate with the anti-corruption agencies in the fight against economic and financial crimes in the public sector. The anti-corruption agencies alone cannot win the fight.

This reference book is intended to aid the anti-corruption agencies in combating economic and financial crimes in public institutions, as well as providing understanding in respect of the critical role of the Internal Audit as the primary source of intelligence gathering of corrupt practices in public institutions. The compilation of incontrovertible evidences for subsequent investigations and successful prosecution should form the bulwark of the work of the Internal Auditors.

Strategic Internal Auditing, anchored on a robust anti-corruption stance is the panacea to check and control corruption.

Agencies must strive to build seamless cooperation to improve capacity and reach. With adequate funding they could migrate to IT-based operations for quicker response in the detection of corrupt practices.

The reference book which is very handy and written in dynamic flex is to be updated with new developments continuously in order to retain focus and sustain attention on the activities of the anti-corruption agencies. It also provides guidance and sharpens the sensibilities of the reader to the machinations of corruption.

This maiden publication discusses in general terms but subsequent editions shall be more specific in detailing of corrupt acts discovered in any institution. It provides a reflective mirror showcasing the decadence in our public institutions, revealing how perpetrators of fraud operate and proffers appropriate remedies that could address the menace. A few may see their reflection and experience change of heart and do what is right for the common good.

Everyone should be encouraged to contribute and say something whenever they see something.

Emmanuel Olisa Iwobi, JP.

CONTENTS

CHAPTER 1

INTRODUCTION

The Nigerian public service was inherited from the colonial service. Nigeria was part and parcel of the British colony until it gained independence in 1960. The administrative authorities then were appointed British officials who owed allegiance to their home government and not necessarily to the Nigerian public.

As a matter of fact, public servants were made to sign the Oath of Secrecy, a doctrine that is generally misconstrued. Oath of Secrecy refers to the extant Public Service rules Nos. 030415-030419 of the Federal Public Service Rules 2008. The spirit of the rule is actually to protect classified information but the general misconception in the minds of many public servants extended the rules to cover even acts of corruption or indiscretion perpetuated in office.

We commend the recent signing into law of the Freedom of Information Act 2011 which invariably would evolve to create more transparency in the manner the public sector conducts business.

The founding fathers in January 1954 unanimously signed and subscribed to the principles of free and independent public service insulated from political control and interference. The spirit was to engender the development of a merit-based people oriented public service. The gains were yet to be consolidated upon when the Nigerian military struck on the 15th of January 1967 and took control of governance. Civil war subsequently ensued between 1967 and 1970.

Altogether, Nigeria experienced six different military interventions in the governance of the country. Of course one does not expect the military to propagate public accountability.

The military government of Nigeria by its monolithic authority dismembered functional public service structure and created the institutions in its own image to serve its purpose.

The military interregnum exacerbated internal contradictions that facilitated corruption in the service. In particular is the promulgation of Decree No. 43 of 1988 which greatly eroded the sense of security and secured future in the minds of public servants. There were distortions in the internal control mechanisms as the supervisory control of the public sector was brought under military political authority. It was an era when employment could be terminated with immediate effect.

Public service became the organizing axis upon which the triangle of misappropriation and misapplication of public funds began. Sudden enrichment of military officers, political office holders and conniving public servants became the bane of the public sector. Military rule significantly entrenched an enabling atmosphere for financial malpractices to thrive unhindered and unchecked for over three decades. The events changed the core values of generations and made sharp practices accepted norm with compulsion to conform. It became an era of intolerance to criticism and aversion to questioning by the governed. The regimes merely represented the interests of a clique, no matter how misinformed or misguided the power holders may have been.

The immiseration of our complex socio-cultural values intertwined with historical events created the fertile ambience for the growth of corrupt practices in all its ramifications. It has now assumed the status of corporate identity having powerful response patterns to ensure self-preservation. The nation is currently facing existential struggles with the retrogressive social phenomenon which has developed and embedded itself in every aspect of our societal fabrics. There is urgent need to inculcate internal detection mechanisms with effective correction process that discourages financial malpractices.

This is against the backdrop of the societal norm that does not accept affluence which source is invisible. If urgent steps are not taken to arrest corruption in our system, it will surely lead to catastrophic consequences. There is need to genuinely assist the current administration in its thrust for transformation in waging strategic war against corrupt activities in every aspect of our polity. Corruption has immensely stunted sustained socio-economic growth and development of the nation.

Despite various well-meaning reforms and establishment of anti-corruption agencies, there is still systemic corruption in both the public and private sectors.

Many analysts and commentators have attributed the failure of requisite development of the country to bad leadership, ill-informed followership or defective constitution as the arguments go. But the truth remains that if corruption is checked in our governance and core values entrenched, every other thing will fall in place.

The Economic and Financial Crime Commission, if adequately empowered, having been in the vanguard in the fight against corruption, is in a vantage position to articulate an effective and efficient approach that will not only eradicate corruption in the system but nip it in the bud wherever it rears its ugly head. Strategic application of adequate resources and public support are the primary pillars in achieving the objectives. Emphasis must be focused on effective monitoring, evaluation and prompt investigation of reported cases. It will definitely check and control the conduct of public servants.

Once the public sector is sanitized, the bandwagon effect will cascade to the private sector and to individuals. The societal pull towards positive direction would ultimately become strong enough to stabilize the system.

This reference book in itself provides invaluable tool in seizing section 6(p) of the mandate of the Commission to sensitize and garner public support and confidence in buying into the vision and mission of the anti-corruption agencies.

Just as the fight against terrorism is everybody's business, everyone should be involved in one way or the other to overcome the scourge of corruption everywhere.

All other agencies involved in fostering good governance must emphasize proper conduct of their staff at all times in order to elicit public trust which is the essential ingredient needed to win the fight against corrupt tendencies.

The agencies include but not limited to the following:

1. Independent Corrupt Practices Commission, ICPC,
2. Code of Conduct Bureau, CCB,
3. Public Complaints Commission, PCC,
4. National Orientation Agency, NOA,
5. Nigeria Customs Service, NCS,
6. Nigeria Immigration Service, NIS,
7. Federal Inland Revenue Service, FIRS,
8. Federal Character Commission, FCC,
9. Office of the Accountant General for the Federation, OAGF,
10. Office of the Auditor General of the Federation, OAGF,
11. National Universities Commission, NUC,
12. Professional Accounting Bodies as ANAN, ICAN and CITN,

13. National Youth Service Corps, NYSC,
14. Federal Civil Service Commission, FCSC.

EFCC is disposed to offering seamless exchange of intelligence and networking towards constructing enduring structure that would facilitate prompt response in nipping corruption before it grows difficult to surmount. We believe that this publication will not only enlighten but would become a watershed in ushering re-orientation in the public psyche and harnessing potentials in building a society based on equity, fairness and accountability.

CHAPTER 2
CORRUPTION

Corruption is an unlawful or immoral conduct intended to secure benefit for one-self or a group. It involves doing things that are dishonest or illegal in order to make money, gain or to keep power or status.

It occurs when by any contrivance a degrading element not in the original plan or design is inserted in the system causing malfunction and ultimately making it incapable of achieving its intended purpose. It is a situation when an individual or group conspires to integrate either for short or long term purposes elements of manipulative character in the structure and functions of an organization not in its original mandate with intent to compel the organs of such organization to serve private ends of personal enrichment other than deliver utility, material welfare and spiritual upliftment of the target public.

The definition above clearly situates corruption in the Nigerian public service and can be viewed also as a breach of trust driven by lower morality or debased integrity often propelled by primordial considerations or poverty.

Federal Government of Nigeria Public Service Rules Nos.030401 and 030402 clearly stipulated various acts of serious misconducts all bordering on corruptive tendencies.

Corruption is wide in context and has both criminal and spiritual implications. The motivations to engage in the act are diverse and can be summarized as either need or greed. It is important to appreciate the different spheres of corruption and place them in proper perspective in order to apply appropriate remedies successfully.

The Nigerian public service comprises of the civil service, judiciary, legislature and all the security agencies. It must be understood that the issues of corruption discussed in this reference book are not limited in part but generally applies to all the aspects of the public sector in Nigeria.

The judiciary in particular which is the last hope of the common man ought not to be tainted with the slightest colour of corrupt acts if the society is to survive.

We are not unaware of the pervading corrupt tendencies in the private sector but the public sector was slated for this manual as the cleaning up of the Augean stable must start from somewhere.

We wish to highlight three main types of corruption;

1. *Petty Corruption*: This is corruption on a smaller scale whereby the lower grades of public servants are engaged in petty stealing or extorting money for services rendered or using their position to gain undue

favour. The motivation is generally need. This level of corruption is generally induced by poverty whereby the acts are justified as means of survival.

It cuts across both public and private sector employments and has become very pervasive in our system, almost like a norm.

In a culture where giving of gifts is like a ritual, it becomes difficult to draw a line between acceptable and unacceptable gift. It makes it very difficult to contain this level of corruption because they can always devise ways to beat the controls. And our people do not hesitate to part with some paltry sum to be given preferential attention.

In some societies, such gifts are regarded as tips, particularly within the hospitality industry.

In other places, they see it as bribe pure and simple and it is discouraged totally. Using a real life experience to illustrate the different views, let me tell a short story of one first time Nigerian ambassador who arrived in Canberra, Australia.

The ambassador and family arrived in Canberra aboard a British Airways flight. As part of the protocol, we were at the airport to receive them. As would be expected, they had so many pieces of luggage for airport clearance. This wonderful Australian porter was happily lending us a helping hand. The luggage was intact as we heaped them on the vehicles to depart for the Residence. Without letting us in, the ambassador dipped into his pocket, brought a 100 dollar bill and was extending it to the porter. The poor porter at the same time was smiling and extending his hand to wave us goodbye. Behold he suddenly realized he was being offered money. He quickly turned and ran away from us.

It was then we had to explain to His Excellency that his kind gesture may be acceptable in Nigeria but not in Australia where it is viewed as a bribe. It was a classic case of culture clash.

The porter was doing the work for which he was being adequately remunerated by his employers. The take home pay of the average Australian worker is enough to cater for the basic needs of the family but that of the Nigerian counterpart may not be enough to take him home let alone feed his family.

You can now see why petty corruption thrives in Nigeria. It is only adequate salary and re-orientation that can change the attitude of the average Nigerian worker to understand that bribery in any form is corruption in itself.

Public Service Rules Nos. 030402(j) and 0304034 nonetheless prohibit bribery and corruption

2. **Grand Corruption:** This is a scale of corruption which occurs at the highest level of government whereby the system is subverted for selfish gains or just to maintain

power or status. Studies have shown that most of the funds that are misappropriated and mismanaged happen at this level of government. The motivation is generally greed. It usually involves outright embezzlement, misappropriation of funds, over inflation of contract sum or other high level fraudulent manipulations.

When a Chief Executive Officer becomes the Chief Executive Thief, it generally spells doom for the organization, as the nuances pervade the entire fabric of the institution. It encourages sycophancy and corruption to take over while transparency and accountability take flight. There is an adage that when the flow of water is polluted at the source, the whole stream is affected.

Grand corruption has been the bane of our public sector for too long. One does not need court convictions to be convinced. The stark reality stares us in the face everywhere you go. In a society where extreme wealth and abject poverty exist side by side, without tangible and commensurate development, something really went wrong.

Corruption over the years has wrought untold hardship to the majority of Nigerians by stifling economic and social services. We are contending with dilapidation of infrastructure, decay in the education sector, dismay in health services, epileptic power supply, unprecedented unemployment of the youths and severe security challenges. People are groveling for mere sustenance and survival.

When the people at the very top are corrupt, the tendency is for the management staff to take undue advantage and that trickles down the line. Manipulation of the process is thus introduced in the system which inherently weakens every control. When people start to steal big time they do not stop. It becomes like drug taken - very addictive. The addict loses the ability to reason. This accounts for mindless acquisition of wealth, by the privileged few, which actually they do not need, only borne out of excessive greed and moral depravity.

Corruption is also the major cause of the inability of many organisations to envision and deliver sustainable projects due to the deviation in focus. Rather, what you have are sub-standard and/or abandoned projects and programmes that we witness all the time. We do not need to cite examples. Many cases abound all over the place.

Grand corruption over the years has contributed to low developmental position which Nigeria occupies in the comity of nations, despite the abundance of resources.

3. *Systemic Corruption:* This is corruption resulting from weakness of the institutions where there is absence

of checks and controls. In Nigeria, we tend to build strong men at the expense of strong institutions. We are generally subservient lot, always giving obeisance to persons in authority even when it is obvious by their actions that they do not deserve it. The culture of "Yes sir" "Yes sir" has permeated all our institutions rendering them ineffective.

The internal contradictions in ethnic and religious affiliations tend to subsume best practices to allow a performance oriented public service to thrive. They cripple positive advancement that would entrench strong bureaucracy.

Instead, parallel administration, incompetence, indolence, eye-service and lackadaisical attitude to work are fostered in the organization. The workers are thus not motivated for team work and do not abide strictly to the Code of Ethics.

All these translate to low productivity with many workers engaged in the provision of services which otherwise could be accomplished by few dedicated and committed staff. The personnel cost of running our public institutions is comparatively astronomical.

In the long past, graduates preferred rather employment in the private sector than government departments. It later changed when corruption manifested in government institutions. People started seeking "lucrative" employments in the public sector.

Such places as the Nigeria Custom Service, Nigeria Ports Authority, National Youth Service Corps of Messrs. Obassa and Kila days, etc became the sought after jobs. The motivation was not necessarily to provide efficient service but to make money. All the various public institutions became weaker and weaker as the manipulation of the systems became the order of the day. It has remained so to this day.

As can be adduced, corruption in the public service has been with us for a long time. Nigeria, since independence, has remained at the level of potentials due to corruption which had negatively impacted on our psyche and institutions.

Fela Anikulapo Kuti was singing about the decadence in the country in the seventies and Nigerians were busy dancing and gyrating to the music, oblivious of the prophetic message contained in the lyrics. The chicken has now come home to roost.

The Economic and Financial Crime Commission under its current leadership could structurally strategize to impact positively and nip corruption in the bud. In this little book we intend to expatiate on the modality of how this could be achieved.

4. ***Other Forms of Corruption:*** In addition to the above classifications, corruption could be categorized based on sectors, viz;

(a) Judicial Corruption,

(b) Police Corruption,

(c) Legislative Corruption,

(d) Political Corruption,

(e) Military Corruption.

All these different categories of corruption are discernible in Nigeria unless we do not want to tell ourselves the truth. How could we survive such monstrous level of avalanche if we continue to live in denial and indolence?

Now is the time for collective action, otherwise the corruption monster is geared to fight back. We have no other country to run to. If we concede defeat, it is then we would realize the disdain many countries harbour against Nigeria. With determination and serious commitment, we shall surely win the fight.

Corruption as can be seen is a very wide subject and covers all aspects of life that detract from perfection or purity. It can be broadly categorized as it affects the public sector.

Our experience as auditors and insiders in the public service revealed that the following specific types of corrupt activities do occur in our public institutions.

These can be attested to by various audit reports, media reports, committee investigations, police and court records, audit queries etc, viz:

1. Embezzlement,
2. Falsification of records,
3. Misappropriation of funds,
4. Misapplication of funds,
5. Bribery,
6. Inflation of contract sums,
7. Stealing,
8. Favouritism,
9. Nepotism,
10. Indiscipline,
11. Drug abuse,
12. Money laundering,
13. Smuggling,
14. Racketeering.
15. Sexual harassment.

We intend to shed some light on the various corrupt acts that stultify effective and efficient service delivery in the public sector. The problem is enormous and diverse.

The Independent Corrupt Practices Commission's (ICPC) mandate covers even a wider range of corrupt activities mainly in the public sector.

The Federal Character Commission ensures equity in the personnel disposition in all public institutions. There are other agencies with their specific functions towards promoting good governance and elimination of corrupt tendencies in the public service.

The general perception is that the fight against corruption in all its ramifications is the exclusive preserve of the EFCC and the ICPC. And that is the way the general public sees it. That is not entirely correct.

The EFCC from inception came into the public psyche as a laudable corruption agency. Many are not even aware of the Commission's specific areas of specialization. They overwhelm the Commission with all kinds of complaints, including issues of civil litigation or matters that should be directed to the regular police force. The Commission is doing a great job albeit methodically and consistently without unnecessary publicity and media distractions.

As financial consultants and erstwhile insiders, we worked closely with the current leadership. The chairman is imbued with professional integrity and dedication to duty. The initiative for this publication was inspired by his style of open administration which seeks to sensitize the public and raise awareness to appreciate the functions of our various agencies and, join forces in the fight against corrupt activities in every aspect of our national life.

A story comes to mind which substantiates the need to create this awareness:

A Nigerian lady working as a nurse in the United Kingdom while the husband lives in Nigeria once came on a visit to Nigeria. In the course of her sojourn in her husband's house, she was relieved of the sum of 3000 Euros. Being anonymously tipped that the husband was planning to marry a second wife, her suspicion that the husband was responsible for the missing money became confirmed in her mind. It took us time to dissuade her, as family friends, that it was not the type of case to be referred to the EFCC but could be settled in-house or at worst the matter could be reported to the regular police within the area. She nonetheless wrote the petition for onward transmission to the EFCC before it was discovered that the mastermind of the theft was their innocent looking house-help who organized the stealing with the connivance of the boyfriend.

There are so many of such cases/petitions inundating the Commission all the time. Section 6 and 7 of the EFCC Establishment Act 2004, specified the functions of the Commission.

CHAPTER 3

PERPETUATION OF CORRUPTION

Now that we have identified the different forms of corrupt activities that militate against effective service delivery in public institutions, it is pertinent to take a closer look at the various ways perpetrators adopt to subvert the system.

It is clear that petty and grand corruption manifest easily when institutions are weak, yielding to systemic corruption. It brings to the fore the importance and urgency required to institute strong checks and controls in all public institutions. Though the rules are there for guidance, some public officers always devise ways to circumvent them for selfish gains.

Strategic auditing becomes the viable solution to mitigating corruption. Unless and until corruption is eliminated, the yearly budgetary items, particularly overhead and capital votes, would never translate to commensurate growth and development in the economy. The predators lurking in the service, blinded by greed and avarice, lie in wait year in year out to pounce.

These perpetrators eventually turn out richer than the institutions entrusted in their care. That is the irony of the peculiar style of governance in our public sector that must be truncated if we shall ever join the global race for rapid development in all spheres.

For enlightenment and guidance, we highlight various risk areas in the management of public expenditure that require careful attention to prevent fraudulent occurrences:

A. APPROVED AMOUNT AND PURPOSE OF EXPENDITURE SHOULD ALWAYS BE CLEARLY STATED

It seems straightforward as stated. But in practice it is not. It is necessary for the approving authority to read and understand clearly memos brought to its attention. If it meets approval, the exact amount approved and purpose for it must be clearly defined, written and dated. It is even more so when the memo requesting such approval covers more than one page. Some unscrupulous subordinates have been known to effect several payments utilizing the approval page, after substituting or altering preceding pages to give impression of different purposes or payees.

Government loses money through such fraudulent payments of which the Chief Executive Officer may not even be aware. It is very important for approving officers to understand thoroughly the vision of the organisation to enable them to align approvals to the attainment of goals and objectives. Where that is not the case, public servants do take advantage with embellished and confusing logic.

Nigeria has come of age for appointments and promotions to be based purely on merit. It is very core in building sustainable institutions to have people in position where they are professionally equipped to discharge their duties.

B. PROJECT APPROVAL MUST BE DISTINCT FROM PAYMENTAPPROVAL

When one fails to imbibe the rules, one may never know when it would be exploited. The execution of a project takes time and stages. There is need for the approving officer to understand the stages and match them to funding within specific time periods. When a project or programme is approved, specific approval for every payment in respect of the project or programme ought to be given at every stage. This helps to monitor and evaluate performance and ensure completion in line with funding.

The Internal Auditor must keep proper records of all payments for the project, particularly when it is paid by installments. The updates of the payments must be sent to the Chief Executive Officer to keep him duly informed. This helps to avoid double payment or payment for project not even executed. Execution of projects is a major critical area of very high risks in respect of financial manipulations and fraud in the public sector.

C.   AVOID AMBUSH TACTICS IN GIVING APPROVAL

A Chief Executive Officer who did not grow through the ranks may never fully understand the machinations and intrigues in the public sector. It is always advisable to take time to understudy the office environment and become very acquainted before taking major decisions.

There are instances in the past when Chief Executive Officers cried foul after giving their approval for payment to be effected. It is very critical to read and understand memos carefully. It is also important to engage the services of a personal assistant who appreciates the intricacies of the job.

Mischievous staff lay ambush to secure approval for projects/programmes where their personal interests were already embedded. Having mastered the nuances and tendencies of the boss, they calculate fortuitous timing to pounce. It saves to be wary when an officer is clutching onto a file preferring to submit it directly and personally for approval instead of using the established communication channel.

D.   CIRCUMVENTING DUE PROCESS
WITH CONTRIVED URGENCY

Perpetrators devise so many tricks. They could deliberately delay acting on a file until the very last minute. At the last moment they resort to fire brigade method as a ploy to circumvent due process. Every other person along the line is whipped into submission. Even the internal audit may be by-passed in the scheme. It happens too often and the aim is always to channel expenditure to areas and persons of interests where personal benefits are already sealed and delivered. Sometimes, awards and payments for capital projects are made on the last day of the accounting year in December without due process while attributing lateness in cash backing under capital vote for the urgency.

The main causes of abandoned projects are traceable to this type of hasty and dubious procurement exercise. The Internal Auditor must endeavour to keep adequate records of the instances where such modes were adopted and draw inferences which would be incorporated into the Audit Report to relevant authorities subsequently.

E. INFLATION OF CONTRACT SUMS

This is the most common fraudulent manipulation. Procurement Act was enacted to stem fraud in the award of contracts but operators negate the spirit of the Act by not adhering strictly to procedure. Blinded by greed and avarice they devise ways and means to circumvent due process. Cronies are engaged to submit multiple bids after giving them insider information and shutting off prospective qualified bidders who otherwise would have enhanced competitive bidding. Advertisement for specific award in line with requirements by the Act are avoided, thereby negating the integrity of the whole exercise from the onset, giving the perpetrators room to pad the contract sum to their whims and caprices.

The very idea of pre-qualification criteria which is to weed out unserious bidders and inculcate professionalism and competence is thus sacrificed. The penchant of subverting competitive bidding in the award of contracts is the kernel in the monumental corruption in the public sector. It constitutes monumental drain in the resources meant for real time development of the country. It clogs the vision for realizing strategic objectives of the organizations as personal interests subsume public interests.

It is commendable now that the Federal Government has introduced Procurement Cadre in the service to replace unqualified persons who either out of ignorance or mischief, pretend not to be conversant with established procurement procedures. It is important too that the Internal Auditor must be very conversant with the Procurement Act and keep track of guidelines emanating from the Bureau of Public Procurement (BPP).

Market surveys are necessary tools at the disposal of the internal auditor in crosschecking and comparing contract sums for guidance. Financial Regulations December 2006 Rules Nos.2936-2950 are very clear on the adherence of due process in public procurement.

F. TRAVEL AND TRANSPORT VOTE

Travel and transport vote is one overhead that is grossly abused in the public service in respect of duty tour allowances and transportation, particularly international airfares. Incidences of approved tours not actually undertaken and accounted for are very common. Nigerians recently witnessed a television programme where some legislators were alleged to have collected estacode and airfares for official trips which they did not undertake.

International travels and estacode add up to monumental expenditure burden for government. Money that could have been utilized in the provision of essential services is wasted on frivolous international junketing. Travel agencies collude with public officers to claim reimbursement of astronomical travel costs. It is a well-known fact that electronic ticket prices issued by airlines are susceptible to doctoring by travel agencies before presenting for reimbursement. And it is usually done with the knowledge and consent of the officer involved in the journey, who also benefits from the inflated prices submitted for reimbursement by the travel agencies.

It is often so bad that you will often find high level public officers who are undertaking journeys in representative capacity for the country, crouching in third class cabin of the aircraft, when actually first class air-tickets have been paid for their journeys.

The act may not be criminally liable but it is morally reprehensible to engage in falsification to profiteer from the same organisation you serve.

The Audit Department must be conscious of the flagrant abuse and verify actual fares paid by the travel agencies on behalf of government by accessing the website of the airlines in question or requesting for the airline authentic receipts before the claim for reimbursement is passed for payment.

It may be advisable in certain instances for public institutions to deal directly with the respective airlines. It will go a long way in reducing the huge overhead cost of international travels as well as ensuring transparency and accountability.

G. **INTERNATIONAL REMITTANCES**

Another area of large scale fraud is manipulation of foreign exchange remittances via the Central Bank of Nigeria (CBN). Institutions that undertake foreign remittances must be wary of managing the risk involved in such transactions. Some dubious staff perfected ploys to defraud the institutions of very huge sums of money. In the public sector, some officers in charge of funds should be watched. It was actually prevalent in the period when the accounts of public institutions were placed with commercial banks.

With the reforms which now places the accounts of public institutions with the CBN itself, it may be difficult to perpetuate such fraud unless with collusion. The banking reforms, including the current cashless policy, have drastically reduced such manipulation in the system. Before now, remittances were a freelance racket for financial fraud in the public institutions that transfer foreign currencies for services overseas.

It was very simple to execute the fraud but very difficult to detect. It could only be unraveled by investigative auditing. It is usually carried out by doctoring the naira exchange component in the duplicate copy of the letter of instruction to the CBN to wire a specific amount of foreign currency. The naira component in the duplicate copy would be increased by simple transposition of just one figure.

The CBN clerk unknowingly stamps the duplicate copy as acknowledgement of the original instruction. The stamped duplicate would then become the source document for raising voucher for both the actual naira equivalent of the remittance. The difference is then pocketed by the perpetrators.

The Internal Auditor may ignorantly rely on the CBN acknowledgement stamp to authenticate the transaction. It may explain the motive behind the Funds Section in the public sector being the exclusive preserve of very few officers in the days gone by.

H. PERCEPTION OF AUTHORITY TO INFLUENCE DECISION

Many public officers are generally cowed by perception of authority which affects decision making as there is usually the tendency to please *"oga at the top"*. Many Internal Auditors are no exception, finding themselves passing dubious payments in order not to displease the *"oga at the top"*. This is a major problem in sustaining strong institutions. You can now understand why major frauds go on in public institutions where there are Internal Auditors who are supposed to be the watchdogs against malpractices.

The reason can be attributed to the virtual lack of independence of the Internal Auditors. This also happens in some government institutions that engage their own Internal Auditors and shun the overtures of the office of the Accountant-General of the Federation to deploy its staff as the head of audit. The independence of the head of Internal Audit should never be compromised at any time to embolden him/her to do what is right at all times.

I. GRANTING OF NON- PERSONAL ADVANCES

The rules regarding granting of Non-Personal Advances for Projects/Programmes are very flagrantly flouted in many public institutions. Financial Regulation No.1402 (iii) is very clear on the procedure and states as follows: "In the disbursement of fund for Non-Personal Advance for Project/ Special Programme, the leader of the Project/Programme shall be the accounting officer and approve payments, while an accountant of appropriate grade shall be attached to the Project/Programme and have the responsibility for disbursement and retirement of the advance". The idea is to prevent abuse by sharing responsibilities instead of a situation when one individual or unit constitutes (a) Initiator (b) Approving Officer and (c) Paymaster, all in one individual or unit.

It is important to understand the cost components of Project/Programme and effect direct payments to the respective payees. It does not add up where huge sums are paid into personal accounts of public officers in respect of government programmes which usually were very shabbily retired and some not retired.

Internal Audit must ensure that the extant rules are strictly followed or file necessary reports without delay.

J.   WAGES AND SALARIES

Before the introduction of the Integrated Personnel and Payroll System (IPPIS), payroll was a government bazaar for doling out money without productivity. Names of cronies of some public officers were smuggled into the payroll for monthly welfare. The problem was that the welfare was always lopsided in favour of some category of persons.

The term "ghost workers" in our lexicon was used in describing this crop of 'workers' who appear only on pay day every month. Payment by cash in respect of salary then facilitated the fraud. IPPIS has no doubt drastically reduced the number of ghost workers through biometric data capturing of the actual staff members.

IPPIS however has its relative risks. It is critically important for the Nominal Roll and Payroll to be in tandem otherwise the gains of IPPIS would be eroded. The responsibility of maintaining the two records used to be under one jurisdiction. But now, the Administration Department maintains the nominal roll while the Accounts Department handles the payroll. Sometimes it leads to conflict in reconciling the criteria for new employments with requisite salary budget and variation to maintain standard.

It behoves on Internal Audit to undertake careful scrutiny of the nominal roll to certify that every new employment followed due process before listing in the payroll. Audit trail of adequate representative sample of the payroll ought to be carried out periodically to guarantee authenticity. It is salient now for all public institutions to migrate to the IPPIS for effective control and realistic budgeting of personnel cost.

K. STORES

Stores is another management risk area that is prone to fraud. Planning efficient store starts with adequate storage capacity. Many public institutions continuously procure store items even when there are no provisions for proper storage and when immediate need do not call for such procurement; just that contract must be awarded before the year runs out.

In some cases payment would be effected without actual delivery of such goods. Some of the deliveries are substandard. You will discover offices littered with various desks, chairs and cloned computers purchased year in year out. It becomes cumbersome to maintain adequate record of store items under such circumstances.

The Internal Audit must wade in to stem the tide. There should be insistence on proper recording of stores in the manner prescribed in the Audit guidelines of 2011.

Appropriate report of the circumvention of extant rules should be made to the Chief Accounting Officer and copied to the offices of the Accountant/Auditor General of the Federation and the EFCC accordingly.

L. CENTRAL PAY OFFICE AND SECURITY DOCUMENTS

The importance of safeguarding security documents in the Central Pay Office need not be over emphasized. Receipt and payment vouchers provide critical information of all the financial transactions undertaken in the public institutions. Future references in respect of every payment could be ascertained from the vouchers as authentic and historical evidence of transactions. There are cases when the relevant files may be missing and these vouchers become the last resort in unraveling all the antecedents to the expenditure.

Adequate security must always be provided in the cash office despite the introduction of the Cashless Policy which made the work of the cashier less risky for fraudulent manipulation.

The Internal Audit must however conduct post auditing to ensure that all transactions in the Cash Book were properly audited. Any transaction reflecting in the Reconciliation Statement after six months must be duly investigated.

M. FALSIFICATION OF RECORDS.

Some public officers, in a bid to retain positions, falsify records. Such records as date of birth, qualifications and achievements are doctored. Many who should have retired changed their date of birth in order to still remain in active service longer than the mandatory number of years. What you then have are people who do not have anything new to offer, who are not in consonance with technological innovations, occupying positions where younger and more vibrant people could fit in for maximum performance.

The Civil Service Commission needs to revive its data base and make them more secure. There ought to be coordination of records of service in such a manner that by the click of a button, detailed information and aggregation of records could be ascertained accurately. Those who are supposed to be retired but connived to stay put should be weeded out.

Situations where retired officers refuse to give way do not add value to the service. There are occasions when you have officers who, by all reasonable assessments, are well over the mandatory retirement criteria, unable even to climb the staircase to their offices, but still continue to hang around, instead of going gracefully and contributing more meaningfully in their local communities.

These are all part of the corruption we are trying to address in the public service.

N. DELIBERATE DUPLICATION OF UTILITY PAYMENT

Officers can sometimes connive to effect and duplicate payments of cumulative utility bills. This is a very crafty fraud that adds up to appreciable sum and drains appropriated funds. The initial payment actually goes to the respective utility company while subsequent payments are converted and siphoned. This type of fraud could be executed where payments are made by cheque or cash and no register of records in respect of monthly settlement of utility bills is kept.

It is always necessary for the Internal Auditors to diligently crosscheck all the payments of utility bills and match them against respective months recorded in a register.

CHAPTER 4

CORRUPTION AND INSECURITY

Nigeria is battling the twin evils of corruption and insecurity. It is important to draw the linkage between corruption and insecurity which tend to reinforce one another where ever they co-exist. Corruption does not exist in a vacuum but is consequential to the premium the society places on the value of life and welfare of others in the distribution of common wealth of the nation. Where there are equity and justice in the process, peace and security are likely sustained. In a situation of injustice, where the dynamics of converting public wealth to private wealth happens in uncontrollable multiples and unchecked, the nation would become self-liquidating entity. The deprivation breeds anger and despair, inducing the willingness of the deprived group or persons to participate in anti-social acts of criminality against the society they belong.

We must understand that the real sponsors of terrorism are the past and present corrupt public officers that looted and are still looting the treasury. Looted funds are slush funds, usually not properly invested but secretly laundered or invested in real estate or phony projects all over the place. They do not really create planned industrial projects for high level job opportunities. It has invariably led to despair and frustration amongst the teeming youths who are unable to find gainful employment. Criminality thus became the only way they know how to survive.

Extremists and ideologues, dressed in religious, ethnic and political garbs are taking advantage and exploiting the situation for selfish gains. It has now degenerated to abduction, murder, kidnapping, rape and all sorts of criminalities never before thought possible in Nigeria.

Everyone who was involved in the plundering of the commonwealth is answerable to the current security challenges in the country. Those public servants, balancing in their small offices and perpetuating all kinds of corrupt practices, misapplying security votes, should realize that they contributed directly or indirectly to the insecurity in the land today.

It is pertinent to appreciate the major causes of the current insurgency represented by the name Boko Haram, which literally translates to "western education is forbidden" originating from the north east of Nigeria. It is on record that the group started out by preaching against police and political corruption in high places. With the prevailing under development of the area and consequent excruciating poverty, it was easy to recruit members against the establishment. The youths with nothing better to do and in hopeless condition were willing to participate in something no matter the gravity or risk involved. Lacking in formal education, they were gullible, easily indoctrinated and susceptible to manipulation.

Boko Haram was founded in 2002 and their leader was subsequently killed extra judicially. The morphed Boko Haram, hijacked and under new leadership of a ruthless ideologue, escalated the perpetuation of all kinds of terror and criminality.

The poor masses being enlisted to execute the evil biddings do not know better, but faithfully carry out orders, in the name of religion or politics or sheer criminality in accordance with the briefing. Some politicians by omission or commission were credited with statements which tended to embolden the perpetrators of terror. International connections and provision of funding from other extremist groups were obviously established making the Boko Haram now very powerful and uncontrollable.

Recent intelligence reports put Boko Haram as the 7th wealthiest terrorist group in the world generating most of its finances locally by kidnapping and robbery. Terrorism in any country can be likened to a bee that found its way into a man's scrotum. It thrives mainly in a dysfunctional and poverty stricken environment. You need to devise smart strategy to expunge it or you end up destroying everything.

It is encouraging that the activities of the group are now being condemned by renowned Islamic clerics both nationally and internationally. The Federal and State governments need to seize the momentum and heighten awareness of the poor masses who have been dangerously indoctrinated. They should as a matter of urgency put in place poverty alleviation projects and programmes that will create alternative opportunities capable of improving the lives of the people.

We commend the recent increment in respect of the mandatory deposit from equivalent of $20,000 to $200,000 as a requirement for the Bureau de Change operating foreign exchange business in the country. It is a very good step in the right direction in mopping up loose cash which facilitates funding of terrorism.

CHAPTER 5

PSYCHOLOGY OF CORRUPTION

S omebody once suggested that there may be need for prospective candidates for public office to undergo psychiatric evaluation in order to determine their suitability. People did not take the suggestion seriously but rather waived it aside.

However, as consultants we got very perplexed by the level of insatiable greed driving people in position of public trust to engage in mindless accumulation of wealth which actually they do not really need. We understand human greed. But greed can be channeled in a positive direction to create wealth, particularly in a capitalist economy such as ours. It is amazing why an officer in the public office could not appreciate and differentiate between personal interest and public interest. It gets even worse when the scheming is all the time to steal from the commonwealth without any consideration of the majority who suffer daily just to get what to eat.

We were constrained to approach few psychoanalysts in Boston, Massachusetts, U.S.A for answers. They were all of the view that the problem of the corrupt minded is not mental but the mind itself. The different driving forces and theories were suggested to us.

One analyst proffered the Freudian Oedipus Complex which is analogous to a situation where an unresolved conflict while growing up deprives someone the benefit of patriotic spirit to the motherland.

If such a person gets into position of authority, that person will plunder the motherland.

Not very satisfied with the theory, we delved deeper. Another analyst suggested the Poverty Complex Syndrome. They explained that there are different forms of psychological disorders driving corrupt minded individuals. The Poverty Complex Syndrome is one that relates to unresolved deprivation at childhood which makes someone to see accumulation of wealth as the ultimate goal in life. Such perpetrators become fixated to accumulate wealth at all costs. The explanations began to make sense to us as to why some public officers will steal and steal and continue to steal. It is ironical that we find such officers living and flaunting lifestyles far above their means while the society watches helplessly with no questions asked.

We received lectures on the difference between Creation of Wealth and Accumulation of Wealth. Creation of wealth, such that people like the Dangotes are doing today, involves brain and hard work which generate real wealth that create employment. Accumulation of wealth is a mere criminal conversion of already created wealth of someone else's efforts and does not add real value to the overall economy of a country.

The paradox of Nigeria's under performance and frightening level of unemployment with the attendant current security challenges is due to accumulation of wealth that were not properly invested.

Public service which ought to be the engine driving development and national integration lost focus in Nigeria when it became an avenue for corruption and accumulation of stolen funds. There is every indication that the bulk of Nigeria's earnings is lost to various corrupt activities.

It was recommended highly that besides security clearance, background checks, bordering on psycho-analytical assessment ought to be adopted as pre-qualification criteria in engaging persons in public service or elective offices in Nigeria. Psycho-analysis has been inculcated in the system of most developed countries, where persons even young or old, exhibiting deviance were counselled and underwent treatments and appropriate rehabilitation.

CHAPTER 6

CORRUPTION AND CONTENTMENT

A one time British Broadcasting Corporation (BBC) survey declared Nigerians as one of the happiest people in the world. Despite bad governance Nigerians find strength and solace in religion. The paradox is sometimes difficult to understand. How can people who are so deprived be so happy? In spite of the appalling environment, majority of Nigerians are hardworking people who are content with whatever they can achieve, given a conducive environment. This underscores the reality that the richest people are not necessarily the happiest people but those with intrinsic contentment in their lives.

Benjamin Franklin aptly captured the truism when he stated that contentment makes poor people rich and discontentment makes rich people poor. This places a large majority of Nigerians in the happy bracket. Corruption drains someone's integrity, without which one becomes shallow and a mere shadow of the real person burdened by conscience. You cannot be happy when you become utterly deficit and lacking in moral fibre.

It is important to realize that money is a means to an end and not an end in itself. When acquired through dubious means, it does not bring self-actualization. You will still remain poor since all you have is money. It does not guarantee you a happy life; neither does it guarantee you a genuine relationship with friends and family. Above all, it does not guarantee you good communion with the Creator.

The Holy Book affirmed that it is easier for the camel to pass through the eye of a needle than for the rich man to enter the kingdom of God. The rich man referred to in the context was the tax collector and the hypocrite who engaged in placing heavy burden on others while they could not lift a single finger to do any good work.

In today's realities, the context applies to corrupt leaders who acquire obscene riches at the expense of the majority whom they swore to an oath to serve but later betrayed. There is need for introspection and sober reflection for those engaged in the betrayal of public trust.

CHAPTER 7

PROLIFERATION OF PARASTATALS

T he Orosanye Report highlighted recently the proliferation of parastatals in the public sector involving duplication of functions. There is need to revisit the report to properly align and restructure these parastatals for effective performance. Many of them have grown into fiefdoms that are not adequately controlled. They were mainly creations of the Act of Parliament which were not subjected to proper oversight of the Federal Civil Service Commission.

The governing council members usually were appointed on ad hoc basis and not fully equipped to appreciate the technicalities of bureaucratic public service. Many of them coming from private sector orientation were more propelled by personal interests rather than public service. What you then have is a group of individuals interested more in sharing contracts and allocating job slots within the organization to themselves. There is no way we can make progress with that type of mindset in the public sector.

Some of the parastatals do not adhere strictly to the federal character principles in the distribution and disposition of personnel or follow due process in the award of contracts. There is usually the tendency to apply primordial prism in the consideration of government policy decisions. Besides the astronomical cost in running these parastatals, many of them have proven to be unviable and just an avenue for corrupt enrichment of individuals.

The nations with people-oriented governments had since discarded patronage-based public service for people-oriented service. There is need to revive the Nigerian public service that is devoid of undue influence and designed for effective and efficient service delivery.

It is ironically ridiculous that the same public servants who cannot give their best to elevate the services at home always prefer to travel abroad and pay for the same services which other societies have laboured to make adequate for their citizens.

Government is advised to take the bull by the horn and order wholesale restructuring of these numerous and moribund parastatals in the interest of the nation.

CHAPTER 8
TRANSPARENCY INTERNATIONAL AND NIGERIA

We are all aware of Transparency International as the global watchdog against corruption with a mission to promote transparency and accountability in governance. One may not always agree with their analysis particularly when it did not favour us as a country. Let us realize however that we live in a global village where perception tends to become reality, particularly when it is coming from a globally recognized institution.

Pronouncements from Transparency International carry a lot of weight and can influence local and international policy decisions and outcome.

Nigeria took the position of 132 out of 133 countries surveyed in 2003 on propensity level to corruption. We were bracketed with countries like Bangladesh, Haiti and Chad as countries with rampant corruption. That was not good for our national image. In 2013, out of 175 countries that were surveyed, we were still down in the rung of the ladder with the position of 144 and in league with Iran.

Although that represented some marginal improvement, a lot still needs to be done to reduce the corruption in our system.

The EFCC under the current leadership is quietly and methodically doing everything possible to strategically fight corruption. The concept of instituting strong internal control in the public sector is part of the strategy.

If the proposals from the deliberations of the National Conference canvassing for more empowerment of the Commission to give it latitude for improved performance could be adopted, it would be very commendable. Especially for speedier trial outcome, it has become necessary to establish special courts dedicated to corruption charges. This would in turn make the ordinary citizen perceive that justice had not only been executed but done in a timely manner.

CHAPTER 9

STRATEGIC AUDITING TO NIP CORRUPTION IN THE BUD

S trategic auditing goes beyond focusing primarily on the appropriate recording of financial transactions but evaluates management processes to identify critical risk areas which hamper the goals of the organisation.

The level of fraud emanating from public institutions calls to question the quality and experience of many internal auditors in public establishments. There is no doubt that capacity building is required to prepare many of them for the 21st century challenges in proper oversight in managing government revenue and expenditures.

Training, designed to inculcate ethical and professional values would serve to ingrain character and competence in the discharge of the enormous responsibilities expected of watchdogs in public environment. The training exercise should be well organised in order to ensure that participants who attended got the full benefits of the programme.

It is traumatizing experience to the public psyche to be exposed to the scale of fraud emanating from public institutions where there are Internal Auditors whose primary functions were to detect and report such breaches early enough to nip them in the bud.

It is really sad that the situation has been allowed to escalate to the scale that is now threatening the corporate existence of our common patrimony.

There is no gainsaying that we require internal auditors who have the requisite training, competence, courage and patriotism to speak out soon enough whenever there are infringements of financial rules wherever they are privileged to serve.

The Economic and Financial Crime Commission, EFCC, and Independent Corrupt Practices Commission, ICPC, do not have adequate personnel and funding to man and police every public institution throughout the Federation. Seamless collaboration, synergy, intelligence sharing, prompt analysis and investigation and unalloyed public support are requisite ingredients to create looming presence of the anti-graft agencies that would pervade every nook and cranny of all governmental institutions to nip corruption in its bud.

Simply put, the above captures the strategic concept, which if properly structured and harnessed, will effectively keep corruption at bay in the public sector.

Corruption thrives because of absolute lack of independent and effective insider oversight. Some of the institutions operate as fiefdoms, having powerful parallel administrations within the formal established administrative structure. The parallel administrations are being teleguided by invisible forces that make real time achievement of public goals illusive by rendering the institutions weak and ineffective.

It engenders the massive corruption that is now being exposed, namely: petroleum subsidy scam, pension scam, police, military and judicial corruption.

All these scams did not start today. It has been the bane of our society for too long. They are being exposed now due to the interventions of the anti-graft agencies, evolution of the social media, communication technology and vibrant civil society groups. They all work together to create the awareness to counter the forces of darkness that has held the country down for too long.

There is no other way to rationalize the state of our current development in the face of trillions of dollars which had been generated all these years and all we can boast of are massive individual properties without meaningful infrastructure and industries that will catalyze and multiply the economy for high level employment generation.

CHAPTER 10

IMPLEMENTATION STRATEGY

The Economic and Financial Crime Commission has a well-equipped training institute in Karu, Abuja, which could be utilized to train specialized audit personnel under the auspices of the Accountant General for the Federation.

These auditors would be deployed to head and oversee all the audit units of the Ministries, Departments and Agencies without any exception. The head of audit must be an officer of equivalent grade comparable to the head of administration otherwise he would be handicapped to report on the shortcomings of the administration. Even states and local governments should key into the system.

The Auditors would be protected and independent since they are not direct employees of the very institutions where they were deployed to serve. They would be mandated to send monthly and extra-ordinary special reports directly to the EFCC, ICPC, Auditor-General of the Federation and Accountant General for the Federation.

Section 6(o) of the EFCC Act confers on the Commission the power to seek such reports from institutions. No new amendments of laws are necessary to demand the information from any public institution. A special department had already been created by the current administration of the Commission that has the capacity to analyze audit reports. Prompt investigative auditing would commence as soon as any discrepancies were observed in any institution. It will definitely make public officers to be circumspect in the discharge of their assigned duties, realising that they are being monitored. It will definitely instill strong checks and control that will make everyone to desist from corrupt practices in the workplace.

The Internal Auditors would be emboldened to do their work, knowing that if any financial fraud emanates from the institution, they would have to bear the blame if it was not reported early enough.

The concept is working in several countries. For instance in the U.S.A, the fear of the Inland Revenue Service (IRS) is well known. Even in the neighbouring Niger Republic, their bureaucracy is strong and there are no short cuts to circumventing laid down rules.

Public institutions are the engines that drive developmental progress and when they are rendered ineffective, progress eludes the society while insecurity and criminality take over the vacuum.

The current leadership of the EFCC on assumption of office admitted publicly that the Commission had some corrupt officers in its fold. The reality led to the establishment of the Department of Internal Affairs, which acts as the guard guarding the guards. That singular initiative greatly sanitized the Commission and placed it on a moral high ground to fight corruption with dedicated and sincere staff.

It is imperative for the Commission to seize the momentum and draw impetus to collaborate with all relevant stakeholders and the public in general to take the fight against corruption to a new level.

CHAPTER 11

INTEGRATED FINANCIAL INTELLIGENCE AND MONITORING SYSTEM - IFIMS

T he Economic and Financial Crime Commission has a Financial Intelligence Unit. The unit can be restructured and empowered to gather, monitor, analyze and process application of financial transactions in private and public institutions to logical ends.

There are many IT based accounting and auditing trends that are making things easier in the private sector. We are all witnessing alerts of banking transactions on our personal phones. In the same vein, financial movements in the public sector can be captured in a blink within the system.

As consultants, we have been pursuing this goal with passion. But it seems there are clogs frustrating the efforts to get the idea running.

We do hope that the EFCC would take up the leadership in embracing the novel idea. The countries with low corruption levels had since embraced the use of technology to prevent fraudulent practices in all their institutions. They appreciate the nature of human greed and avarice that thrive in weak institutions where opportunities are available to play to selfish advantages. Technology makes it very difficult for people to manipulate policies.

If the will is there, politically and professionally, technological auditing will become the last bastion in eliminating undue influences in policy implementation and eradicating financial corrupt practices in the Nigerian system.

The government has already embraced laudable IT based applications to improve management of public expenditure such as Integrated Personnel and Payroll Information System, IPPIS, Government Integrated Financial Management Information System, GIFMIS, Treasury Single Accounts, TSA, but there is still a missing link. The missing link is the integration of the IT based auditing, IFIMS, to fish out manipulative garbage in the system being introduced by human elements.

Treasury Single Accounts which was introduced to stem the collusion between public and private institutions to manipulate government funds is already being circumvented in some quarters. Some have devised means of paying out huge sums from the treasury single accounts back into commercial banks in the guise of project or operational funds. In this way, proper monitoring and supervision become slack and proper accountability could not be done.

It is for this reason that IFIMS becomes inevitable. It will become the final solution which we make bold to say is very achievable. The blueprint is already available and has been demonstrated. It will greatly broaden and fasten the scope of financial surveillance capable of monitoring movements of funds in Nigeria. It must be realized that slush funds looted and in possession of disgruntled elements constitute the bulk of the Boko Haram financing. Intelligence reports from the United States clearly stated as much. Cutting off the channels of funding to Boko Haram would greatly weaken their capacity to strike.

IFIMS will not only entrench strong internal control mechanism in the public service but is situated to providing intelligence that anti-corruption agencies could use to nip money laundering and other financial manipulations in the system.

CHAPTER 12

CONCLUSION

We exhort people to see this publication as a humble invocation to patriotism and call to positive action on the part of all to work together to rescue the country from the grip of the few powerful individuals who are subverting the system and refuse to change. These perpetrators must be made to comprehend the danger facing the nation. It will not augur well for anyone should Nigeria collapse. We strongly believe that we shall overcome this phase in our march to nationhood if we all eschew selfishness and greed and work diligently for the common good.

It does not profit any one to gain the whole world at the expense of one's soul. The truth remains that some of those who contributed in wreaking havoc on Nigeria are in the twilight of their sojourn and would soon be called to final account. Some of them are already dead.

Besides the criminality of corruption, the act degrades the value system and traumatically affects people. Corruption is also sinful and has spiritual implications. However one sees it or whatever one calls it - injustice, impunity, insatiable greed or indiscipline negates development.

It is only attitudinal change and the elimination of corruption in our psyche and system that can usher integrated and real time economic development in Nigeria. It is time for all people of goodwill to speak out and condemn corruption in its entirety and join forces with our security network to fight the twin evils of corruption and terrorism to a standstill. It is no time for apportioning blames or pointing accusing fingers either to past administrations or even to colonial Britain. We should take our destiny in our hands. There is a limit to what international assistance can achieve for us.

The country belongs to all of us. Everyone should enlist and contribute in whatever way possible to overcome the current challenges. The social media, civil societies, market and town unions, trade unions should continue to demand accountability, probity and transparency in governance. The public service is not a cult but public trust where information should be accessible so far as it does not border on national security. Let it be clear that for instance the emoluments paid to public officers at whatever level do not in any way constitute security risk except where there is something to hide. We should be determined to shun all forms of evil that tend to undo and obliterate our dreams for a prosperous and egalitarian Nigeria.

Peace, justice and accountability constitute the tripod upon which sustainable growth and development thrives in any society.

In other words, political stability, vibrant public sector and competitive private sector are necessary to drive prosperity of a nation.

www.ingramcontent.com/pod-product-compliance
Lightning Source LLC
Chambersburg PA
CBHW030526290526
45786CB00004B/1638